History
Ming Dynasty

© **Copyright 2019 by Dinobibi -All rights reserved.**

The contents of this book may not be reproduced, duplicated, or transmitted without direct written permission from the author.

Under no circumstances will any legal responsibility or blame be held against the publisher for any reparation, damages, or monetary loss due to the information herein, either directly or indirectly.

Legal Notice:

You cannot amend, distribute, sell, use, quote, or paraphrase any part of the content within this book without the consent of the author.

Disclaimer Notice:

Please note the information contained within this document is for educational and entertainment purposes only. No warranties of any kind are expressed or implied. Readers acknowledge that the author is not engaging in the rendering of legal, financial, medical, or professional advice. Please consult a licensed professional before attempting any techniques outlined in this book.

By reading this document, the reader agrees that under no circumstances is the author responsible for any losses, direct or indirect, which are incurred as a result of the use of information contained within this document, including but not limited to errors, omissions or inaccuracies.

Contents

4

Introduction

Imagine a time when computers, automobiles, and other modern conveniences did not exist. China is one of the longest settled areas of the world; therefore, inventions, art, culture, and society have changed multiple times and in many` ways from the beginning of Ancient China to now. A time existed when people focused on trade expansion, the unification of a nation, fighting interlopers (invaders), and making life easier with new inventions. Modern societies still focus on trade expansion, unification, invaders, and inventions, including modern China. Early Chinese dynasties shaped the current society and economics of China. The Ming Dynasty is only one dynasty of twelve dynasties in China. The Ming Dynasty advanced trade expansion, inventions, art, and culture.

As you explore the Ming Dynasty, you will discover:

- What life was like at the beginning of the Ming Dynasty
- Aspects of the world up to and including the Ming Dynasty
- The government structure

- The social structure
- The period
- Geography of the dynasty

You will explore basic information about the Ming Dynasty, including who the rulers were, how and why the dynasty ended, and the goals of the dynasty.

At the end of this short guide, you will understand the

- Important inventions and discoveries
- Religion
- Art and culture
- How the Ming Dynasty impacted today's society

Setting the stage for your understanding of the Ming Dynasty requires an understanding of China's beginning through the last ruling dynasty. The timeline and the geography of the Ming Dynasty will help you put the rulers, major events, inventions, and culture into perspective, and lead to your complete understanding of how the Ming influenced today's society.

Chapter 1: Background Information on the Ming Dynasty

Archeological digs show habitation, in what we call China, began circa 2000 BC. Scholars call this the Xia Dynasty. Some dynasties would last over five hundred years, and others, only a hundred. The Chou, or Zhou, Dynasty (1045-771) split into the Western and Eastern Zhou, splitting China between several leaders. In 771 BC, the Western Zhou fell; however, China remained split between state alliances. A change came in 221 BC when Qin reunified the country. Qin Shi Huang named himself the first emperor of China and decided to build one long wall. Walls were built starting in the 7th century BC, and the walls blocked easy paths into China. During the State of Qi, "Great Wall" was used as a moniker. The Song Dynasty came after the State of Qi.

Genghis Khan

The Yuan Dynasty (1279-1368) started two years after Genghis Khan died. Genghis Khan, a Mongol leader, explorer, and warrior, tried to overtake China and several Western countries but failed to rule China. His grandson, Kublai Khan, would be the one to succeed in ruling China by overthrowing the Song Dynasty and starting the Yuan Dynasty. Relocation of the capital occurred from Nanjing to Beijing. Khan, now called Shizu, opened Western trade along the Silk Road and by sea, through Marco Polo, an Italian merchant. Khan's relatives kept Mongol rule in China, until a peasant, Zhu Yuanzhang, rose against the Mongols.

Kublai Khan

Zhu Yuanzhang was born in 1328, to peasant parents, who lived near the Yellow River. Zhu was 16 when a series of natural disasters flooded the river, and his parents died of a disease. Zhu went to live in a monastery; however, Buddhist monasteries required payment, and when his money ran out, Zhu was forced to leave. He begged for food until he was 24 and with enough money returned to the monastery. Zhu learned to read and write, something most peasants were not allowed to do.

Yuan troops came through the area, burning and destroying the monastery. Zhu survived and joined a rebel group. At 30, Zhu led the Red Turban Rebel Army. In 1356, his army conquered

10

the old capital, Nanjing. Strategically, Nanjing was an important city for accessing the Yangtze River and southern China. Nanjing became Zhu's capital. For ten years, Zhu Yuanzhang led his army into battle, attacking Beijing (known then as Dadu) in 1368. Zhu and his army defeated the Yuan, sending the court back to Mongolia and Yunnan. Yunnan was the only part of China, the Mongols continued to hold, until 1380.

Zhu Yuanzhang's defeat of the Yuan in Beijing began the Ming Dynasty and his reign as Emperor Hongwu. He died in 1398; however, his policies became imperative to Ming rule. Emperor Hongwu kept Nanjing as the capital but ensured his army protected the northern border against Mongol invaders.

Important Events During the Ming Dynasty

- Emperor Hongwu ordered the Great Wall rebuilt.
- 1371: Emperor Hongwu banned maritime trade and re-instituted the imperial tributary system. He wanted to end pirate attacks. Foreigners could not enter China unless they were part of the tribute system.

- 1401-1424: Emperor Yongle reversed the trading ban and started the construction of the Forbidden City (see details in Chapter 3).

Emperor Yongle

- 1407: Under Emperor Yongle, Chinese troops invaded Vietnam and took over ruling the country.
- 1408: Completion of the *Yongle Cannon*, the most comprehensive encyclopedia
- 1415: Reconstruction of the Grand Canal began, increasing trade between Shandong to the mountains.

Grand Canal

- 1420: The construction of the Forbidden City is complete, and the capital moves to Beijing.

Forbidden City

- 1428: Le Loi defeats the Ming, taking Vietnam back.

Le Loi

- 1449: Emperor Zhengtong is kidnapped by Mongols for four years, with no ransom ever paid.
- 1514: Trade opened in South China to Portuguese traders.
- 1557: Portugal gains Macau (an island) for a colony.
- 1578: The world's first medical textbook, *Compendium of Materia Medica*, is finished, listing 18,000 Chinese medicines and 11,000 formulas for treating diseases.
- 1601: Matteo Ricci, a Jesuit (Roman Catholic priest) was allowed into the capital, when most foreigners were not. Ricci brought Catholicism to China.

Matteo Ricci

- 1628: Li Zheng, another peasant with an army, rebelled against the grain taxes.
- 1642: The city of Kaifeng is flooded by Ming Army tactics, killing every Kaifeng resident.
- 1644: Li Zicheng, a Manchu leader, takes his army to Beijing and breaks into the city. Emperor Chongzhen commits suicide, and the Qing Dynasty starts. The Qing Dynasty (Ch'ing) lasted until 1911.

Geography of Ming China

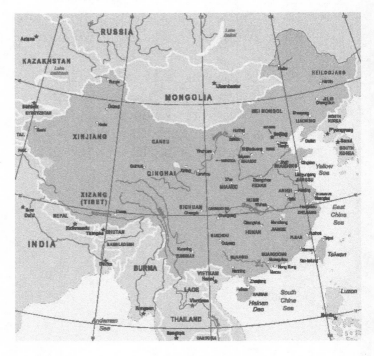

China Map

Ancient China is the same size as today, although the British once ruled Hong Kong, and Taiwan still fights for independence from China. Macau is also back under Chinese rule; Portugal left during the Qing Dynasty. China's borders are North Korea, Russia, Mongolia, Kazakhstan, Kyrgyzstan, India, Nepal, Bhutan, Burma, Laos,

Vietnam, and the South and East China seas. Russia borders China in two places; however, the area between Mongolia and Kazakhstan is extremely insignificant compared to the border on the northeastern side. India also has a long border with China, split by Nepal and Bhutan.

China has deserts, plains, and mountain regions. Manchurian and North China are plains. The Gobi Desert is partly in Mongolia, creating a vast border and treacherous landscape. Other desert areas included Ordos and Taklamakan. For mountainous regions, there is the Plateau of Yunnan, Plateau of Tibet, Kunlun Mountains, and Tien Shan. The Himalayan Range, including Mount Everest, borders China.

Kunlun Mountains

Seas and Waterways

On the east, the Pacific Ocean borders China, along with the East and South China Seas. The Yellow and Yangtze rivers are most important for trade and agriculture, particularly so during the Ming Dynasty. The Yellow River, or the "cradle of Chinese civilization," is 3,395 miles long, putting it as the sixth longest river in the world. The Yangtze River is the third longest at 3,988 miles. The Yangtze River was once a boundary between north and south China.

Yellow River

Summing up the Period

China showed strength in military and government, enough to continue to outlast the occasional invading forces, the ruling Mongols, and interrupting sea trade. Civilizations around the world created inventions to travel by land and sea, to explore other parts of the world, and eventually understood the world was round. Like Europe, Roman, and Ottoman empires, the caste system flourished during the Ming Dynasty, with one main ruler and advisors to help the emperor make decisions.

Periods of war and peace, coupled with overturned social thoughts, would improve or worsen people's survival and positions in society, enough to cause hope and despair. Lessons taken from daily life, the laws established, and government structure help us understand why the Ming Dynasty ended.

Chapter 2: Life and People

We know during the Mongol rule, China was separated into four classes. The lowest class was merchants, and then farmers. Artisans and nobility came next, respectively. The Ming Dynasty helped city life become more important, allowing for further economic and urban development. The class system may have changed during the Ming Dynasty; however, distinctions existed.

Class by Occupation

Occupation defined the classes: Shang, Nong, Gong, and Shi.

Shang

The Shang were merchants, and as the lowest class, they could not wear silk or ride in carriages. Traders by birth, merchants transported goods and food made by the Nong and Gong. Merchants could buy land to gain respect; however, the higher classes felt greed motivated them and not any contribution to a better society. The Ming Dynasty was influential in changing the perception of merchants, where more common people started businesses and contributed to China's economic development.

Nong

Due to contributions of food to the empire, the peasant farmers had more standing in Chinese society. Farmers produced the food; therefore, farmers were productive and active members who also kept the Emperor and higher classes alive through farming.

The Nong lived outside cities in small villages of a hundred families. The Nong worked family farms and provided food to pay for their taxes. Each male peasant farmer would serve one month of the year in the government. The work could be military or construction related. Farmers assigned to construction worked on the canals, palaces, city walls, or the Great Wall of China.

Great Wall of China

Peasant farmers farmed rice or millet, depending on their location; the southern provinces grew rice. Wealthier farms raised goats, pigs, and chickens and had dogs or oxen to help in the fields.

Tea (Cha) was also farmed as a beverage for the elite classes. Tea was discovered centuries before the Ming Dynasty but became imperative to trade for western cultures at the height of sea trade.

The food provided for sale and trade was seasonal based on the time of year and what would grow in the fields. Fallow land caused struggles for farmers and city dwellers, sometimes limiting food supplies, during the Ming Dynasty.

Gong

The Gong had skills to make society better; as artisans and craftsmen, the Gong were either private or government employees passing their skills down to their offspring. In later Ming, the Gong worked in factories to share their artistic talents with the world by creating many artistic pieces, including Ming vases. Ming vases are porcelain with white and blue paint. Decorative designs in blue paint were typically flowers, but some of the unique vases tell stories of daily life.

Antique Chinese under glazed blue and white wine jar

Shi

The Shi was an elite class, just under the Emperor. Many officials came from the Shi class during the Ming Dynasty and were aristocrats who entered the bureaucratic wheel. The Shi had the privilege of riding command· in battles. The Shi represented wisdom and education by becoming scholars who went into government positions or held standing among their peers.

The Shi were privileged to attend a school or have a scholar come to a noble's home. Shi learned to write using calligraphy and studied Confucius' teachings and poetry. Poetry and Confucius' beliefs, government, and philosophy were considered important skills for any government official.

Confucius

Confucius, or Kongqiu, (551-479 BCE) is the most famous Chinese scholar, philosopher, and politician. Confucius' teachings still influence civilization in East Asia, including politics. Confucius lived a plain life built from self-cultivation—an ability to shape his life and destiny—to become an important figure. In China, Confucius is called Kongqiu, but Europe uses the spelling Confucius, calling his teachings Confucianism.

Kongqiu was most likely part of the aristocracy, but his family was poor by the time Kongqiu was born. Personal writings tell us Kongqiu wanted to learn and strove to do so becoming a young scholar. Kongqiu had only minor government jobs, such as managing stables and bookkeeping before nineteen. By thirty, Confucius was considered a brilliant teacher, educating anyone who would listen. Kongqiu established the career of teaching and believed in training "exemplary" people through self-improvement and social interaction. Public service was considered integral to any true education. Kongqiu wanted to be active in politics to spread his ideas of humanism. By the age of forty and into his fifties, Confucius was a magistrate, assistant minister, and a minister of justice. Kongqiu's political career was short, but his loyalty to the emperor ensured Kongqiu was part of the inner circle, providing moral teachings. However, by 56, Kongqiu was not politically useful, so he went into exile.

During Kongqiu's exile, he wrote about his life, his thoughts, morals, and political concepts. Confucius preserved the classical traditions by editing and writing. Confucius died at age 73, leaving behind his legacy and his writings; the writings are must-reads for anyone studying Chinese culture, history, and politics.

Kongqiu lived hundreds of years before the Ming Dynasty, but Kongqiu's lessons transcended his abilities. The Civil Service Exams during the Ming required an intimate knowledge of Confucius' teachings even though much of the Ming Dynasty thoughts contradicted Kongqiu's teachings and morals.

School Life in Detail

State schools, modern-day elementary schools, had four levels and required students to pass the first level before moving to the next and eventually finish all four. People had access to Imperial colleges when all four levels of the school were complete, and created the system where only certain children of officials could attend, such as 5th rank officials and higher. Little changed from the establishment of schools around the first century AD to the end of the Qing. Some schools existed in name only, but others cropped up such as the Painting Academy during the Ming Dynasty.

The Ming Dynasty had two forms of private schools: academies paid for by country gentlemen and Sishu (private schools) provided by scholars.

The Ming Dynasty evolved when it came to school life, but not enough to change the ranking nobility gained above the lower classes.

The Civil Service Exams, or Ke Ju, could be taken by anyone, and the highest scorers would gain the best jobs. A person could try more than once to pass because the exams would mean a job as a government official with a rank assigned. However, the Emperor and his staff exerted control over what people could learn, especially among commoners. The exam followed Confucius' teachings and poetry based on the current rulers' thoughts. Any step out-of-bounds meant persecution for heretical thoughts.

The Chinese alphabet has 3,000 characters. Emperors ignored requests to create a simplified version of the language to keep lower classes from becoming educated. Emperors thought more educated people would lead to a threat to the throne.

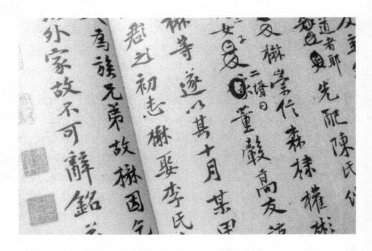

Chinese pictograph, calligraphy tablet of Huang Tingjian

Emperor Hongwu's peasant life could have gone differently, had he not had access to scholars and education through the monasteries. Hongwu might have been as uneducated as others in his class. For those who sought education, had the correct societal ties and money, private learning was available.

Family Life in China

China is a patriarchal society, where three generations shared a home: grandparents, parents, and children. If the father died, his son would take over providing for the home and ensuring his mother retained respect. Respecting the elders was paramount in Chinese culture, even after death. Ceremonies, on their death day and birthday, showed respect to elders.

Parents would arrange marriages, often seeking a better or equal social standing. The children had to obey their father on all points.

Chinese multigenerational family portrait at home

The wife was given household status based on her marriage position. The main wife took care of the house, the expenses and coffers, and hired servants. They also raised the children. Concubines, or additional wives, could garner favor with the father; however, they rarely gained more standing than the first wife. The wives had a caste system, and machinations (tricks) could unsettle the ruling wife to the point of death.

Women and Social Standing

Women were considered less valuable. They were traded in marriage to gain social standing or favors. Nothing was wrong with abandoning a female baby on the streets, leaving the poor child to die. Few high-class families educated their daughters, leaving most women uneducated. Chinese women bound their feet because small feet were considered proper, so many women were unable to walk correctly.

Village Life

Ninety percent of the Chinese lived in villages during the Ming Dynasty. The villages ranged in size from fifty to one hundred families, and smaller villages existed in the north. Inter-village marriage was highly acceptable to avoid incest taboos, creating close relations with other villages. Trade between marriages shifted from the barter system to money. Peddlers would go from village to village selling wares and providing news and gossip. Entertainment was not important because work took most of the villagers' time. Rural life was bustling with activity from regional fairs hosted by monasteries to markets. At least once a year, traveling theater troupes would come through the villages.

City Life

City life meant hundreds of thousands of people living behind walls, where gates would be closed and locked at night, preventing travel after dark.

Activities in the city increased in comparison to village life. Entertainment was necessary, with traveling troupes, theater, places to drink and eat, and more festivals.

Fengshui and numerology made up urban planning. Fengshui states buildings, shrines, and even furniture need to balance. Numbers in China, such as three, five, and nine held significance. People arranged cities based on beliefs in Fengshui and numbers. Local features such as stars, bodies of water, and compass direction determined the orientation of buildings. City planners divided the city and fields into nine sections, all identical in size.

Three Zen Stones and Circles

The creation of cities determined the homes and markets. Slaves lived in quarters at wealthy homes, while servants had homes in the servant quarters of the city. Slaves or servants shopped for the food, made the meals, and ran errands for their employers. Depending on the emperor, slaves were executed without retribution from the law. Slaves were traded, sold, or ended up in servitude to the crown.

Separate market areas for food and goods existed. Merchants sold jewelry, imported goods, and other high-class items at the markets to the nobility. Merchants had to bow with respect and hold licenses to operate. Merchant wares sold on tables in the market, and some merchants had shops with roofs. Medicine, books, and furniture sold in shops versus on the street tables.

Servants or slaves would go shopping with their mistresses. Men held the money but often provided a stipend to their wives and concubines for trinkets or household items.

Home Construction

Many homes were structured around a courtyard, surrounded by rooms, leaving the yard open to the sky. Kitchens were separate from the main house. The hall was a place for furniture and living space. Furniture included chairs and tables in the hall, and beds called Kang in the bedrooms.

The traditional Chinese courtyard of a historical house

Kang beds were on platforms where fire, hot water, or air could heat the beds. Studying was the only other time people used furniture.

The Gong and Shi classes had more spacious homes. The merchant class, as they rose in society, could gain some of the finer things like furniture. The Nong had square homes surrounding courtyards, but they did not have as much furniture or palatial Kang beds.

Religion

The Ming Dynasty was mostly Buddhist; however, Daoist, Jesuit, Islam, and Muslim religions started entering China. Villages had shrines and temples, and monks would conduct pilgrimages to spread religion. Ceremonies occurred at home with a small shrine to ancestors. Family members hosted rituals on the first and fifteenth days of the month, special occasions, and birthdays with the eldest male heir conducting the ceremonies. These rites are still done today.

Buddhism originated in India. Before Buddhism's arrival, the Chinese believed in Dao or Taoism, a philosophy coined by Lao-Tzu circa sixth century BC. The philosophy advocated religious piety and humility, with a focus of living in harmony.

Lao-Tzu statue

Confucianism is a form of government and philosophy many people associate with religion. From a religious viewpoint, the social values, and emphasis on trust and helping others fit Confucianism into religion and a way of life.

Christianity arrived in China during the later Ming Dynasty, and although accepted today, the religion was guarded against, even disregarded by the emperors, to the point that if someone wasn't practicing Chinese religions and beliefs he or she would be executed.

Holidays and Festivals

The people held three big holidays during the Ming Dynasty. The first was the Lunar New Year, Xin Nian, a festival starting in late January and going through early February. Chinese still celebrate Lunar New Year today. Peasants would use drums, gongs, and firecrackers to frighten away "beasts." The festivities included writing poetry, visiting relatives, serving special food, and dancing. Tales of folk heroes, dismissal of evil spirits, and paying off debts were part of the festival to bring in a better and safe New Year. On the fifteenth day of the festival, there is a Lantern Festival to celebrate the first full moon of the first month.

Bang the Drum

Dragon Boat Festival is an ancient ceremony which continues today. The festival occurs in the sixth month of the lunar calendar. The festival is meant to control the rivers, bring more rain, and provide a healthy season for growing. The festival is about food, weather, and boat racing.

Dragon Boat Festival

The third festival is the Autumn Moon, which honors the harvest. The festival happens during the eighth month. During the full moon, adults drink rice wine and create poetry, while children light lanterns. Emperor Hongwu used the festival before his rule to pass messages through mooncakes to encourage a revolt against Mongols. Mooncakes are a baked dessert made with flour, syrup, and flower seed or fruit paste. The paste uses fruits, seeds, or crushed flower petals to create a thick filling or jam-like spread.

Mooncakes and tea

The Twenty-Four Seasons, based on the sun's journey, the solstices, and equinoxes marked events. Peasants and city people would check the moon and sun cycles and gave names to each important seasonal phenomenon.

Clothing

Clothing marked status, where certain colors were illegal to wear unless you were the emperor. The emperor, empress, court ladies, and civil and military personnel had formal and daily clothes. Lower classes only had one style.

Commoner clothing for women included hemp or cotton outfits. Layers kept women warm during the cold months. The outer layer was a long skirt, wrapping around their chest to tie in place and cover their ankles. Over the skirt was a short coat, going to the waist that wrapped around the front, tying right over left in the front.

Women's undergarments included pants to ensure if the wind blew the legs would be warm and unseen by men. Men wore pants covered with a longer shirt than women had but also wrapped around right over left. These shirts resembled tunics.

Servant clothing

Men in government positions wore silk covers, typically, one long cover with bell sleeves wrapped right over left, without patterns. Formal wear included patterns, never dragons or other emperor symbols. Emperors had the most decorative silk gowns, with more moderate silk under covers for relaxing or being with their consorts.

Noble and affluent women would wear skirts like the moonflower skirt, which had ten pieces of fabric, in a pleated style, so if the girl spun around, it would look like a flower. Formal wear had the grander sleeves, often accompanied by wraps or shawls of embroidered silk. Noble women wore scented pouches, jade pendants, and other jewelry items around their waist.

Officials wore a black silk hat and black round-collared robe signifying their position. The outfit would have a leather belt. Officials wore specific colors to show affiliations, positions, and rank. Birds, like egrets, would be stitched into the fabric as signs of their rank.

Military professionals had armor, made of thick leather, helmets, and swords for wars, but they wore robes when walking around garrisons or other stations.

Military clothing

Jade was significant to rank for both men and women. Ming and other dynasties' people thought jade could protect them, so jade was worn as a talisman and to show their station in life. Artisans embedded pearls, jade, emeralds, rubies, opals, and sapphires in hairpins, sculptures, rings, earrings, crowns, and headdresses. The more elaborate headdresses, crowns, and pins showed wealth.

Art

Poetry, music, drama productions, and creative arts marked a period of indulgence for emperors and high-class citizens. Porcelain became more sophisticated with glazed designs, showing intricate scenes. Vases might show flowers, animals, and revered creatures like the Phoenix, or city life. The lacquer carvings displayed by wealthy families used the items to show off their status and respect for art. Furniture, writing, and decorations became part of the appeal in a home's décor.

Painting techniques changed, increasing from the Yuan and Song periods, to include many of the most renowned painters of Chinese history. Qiu Ying, Shen Zhou, and Wen Zhengming were the most famous painters. Their skills were in demand by emperors, nobles, and aristocrats. Qiu Ying earned six pounds of silver for a scroll created for a wealthy person for gift for his mother's birthday.

Medicine

The Ming Dynasty marked medical advancements, such as inoculation. Inoculation, or variolation, is a shot to prevent disease. Credit for the first smallpox vaccination goes to China. Western science credit Edward Jenner with the invention (1796), but a form of the vaccine existed during the Ming Dynasty.

Acupuncture, a method of using needles to stimulate or relieve nerves was prevalent during the Ming Dynasty.

Forms of Chinese medicine revolved around proper diet, nutrition, and foods found to improve health, such as circulation (blood flow), heart troubles, and disease.

Chapter 3: Ming Dynasty's Government and Emperors

The Ming Dynasty was a monarchy lead by the Emperor. The royal family was significant because the first-born son, if he survived, would take over ruling when the emperor died. The government system had three departments and six ministries during most dynasties. The Ming only had one institution – the secretariat. Other dynasties had the Chancellery and Department of State Affairs. Emperor Hongwu allowed the Secretariat to remain as a department for drafting policies. The Chancellery reviewed policies, which is why Emperor Hongwu abolished the Chancellery during the Ming. Reviews of Hongwu's policies did not occur. The Department for State Affairs was responsible for implementing policy, and Hongwu wanted sole discretion, thus ending the department.

The six ministries remained, but the Emperor had direct control over all directors of the ministries. In 1430, a change to the government system occurred, bringing back the Censorate. The Censors had a direct line to the Emperor. As bureaucrats, the Censors provided suggestions to the Emperor based on information from traveling inspectors sent to oversee provincial administrators. Censors could impeach an official if the official did not do the job correctly.

The Emperor had Grand Secretaries who would help with the paperwork. Their job was to coordinate between the six ministries: Personal, Rites, Revenue, Justice, War, and Public Works. The Ministry of Personal covered works relating to employees, including promotion and work assessment. The Ministry of Rites handled ceremonial issues. The Ministry of Revenue collected tax, handled state revenues, and currency.

The Ministry of War oversaw couriers and armed forces. The Ministry of Justice handled judicial matters including the penal process, but they could not exert power over the Censors. The Ministry of Public Works oversaw construction projects and roads and standardizing weights and measures.

Historically, China had a streamlined government based on merit rather than connections which arose during the Ming Dynasty. China prospered under certain Ming Emperors due to the government's efficiency.

Hongwu's Reign

Emperor Hongwu established government policies, including limiting the power of certain people in the palace and restructuring the government. Hongwu took away eunuchs' power because they took part in internal politics. Eunuchs were peasant men who gave up their ability to have children to serve the emperor. Their authority made the court highly decadent, and their power could challenge the Emperor. Hongwu created a centralized authority restricting eunuchs' positions by removing eunuchs from state affairs and keeping illiterate men in the palace.

Hongwu accepted Neo-Confucian officials who passed the imperial exams. The men depended on the court to provide positions. The emperor rewarded intelligence, education, and loyalty.

Emperor Hongwu created a private military institution called the Embroidered Uniform Guard. The group of secret police would spy on his subjects and, if necessary, assassinate those who planned against the emperor.

Paper Currency

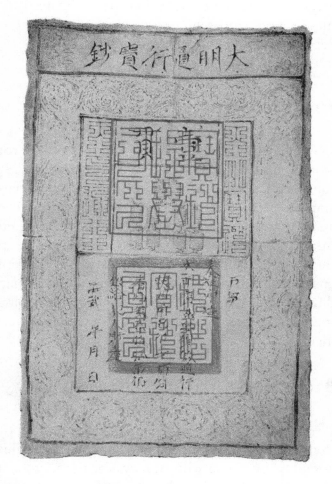

Money

Money existed before the Ming Dynasty; however, Emperor Hongwu built on the invention of currency, using paper instead of metal. Unfortunately, starting the concept of paper money caused inflation by too much being in circulation.

Pro-Peasant

Given Hongwu's background, the Emperor worked to eliminate slavery and starvation. He ruled with a heavy hand when it came to officials and the rich. He created public works projects and gave peasants land. Any peasant who could turn fallow land to a producing farm would keep the property and not be taxed. The concept ensured there was more cultivated land than during other dynasties. Peasants prospered, going to cities to sell their goods, and the population increased.

Merchant Policy

Peasants often became slaves, being exploited by the officials and rich, making Hongwu focus his attention on those with money like the merchant class. He enforced higher taxes for merchants, relocated several merchants, and banned sea travel. Despite his attempts, the merchant class did not shrink, and commerce grew, often due to overpopulation and poor soil. People had to leave China and start finding their money through trade. Merchants traveled the Silk Road during the sea ban, which led to increased travel along the Silk Road. Trading was imperative to the survival and growth of the Chinese government.

Massacres

Hongwu is said to have killed hundreds of thousands of men. Anyone who challenged his reign, who might plan a rebellion or coup, was killed by his special police. One legend says a scholar gained an audience with the emperor, berated Hongwu, but was smart enough to bring his coffin, but Hongwu did not kill him.

We credit Emperor Hongwu with establishing spies, paper money inflation, overpopulation, growth, and development. Many of the policies he established continued after his death. Hongwu started drafting legal codes to be more comprehensive and intelligible, to prevent officials using unclear language for loopholes. The Da Ming Lu, or Code of the Great Ming, was an improvement to the Tang Dynasty Code, ensuring emphasis on family relations, improvement of treatment towards slaves, and making sure slaves, and free citizens were protected. Before the Ming, executing a slave without any sanction on the killer was acceptable. Slaves were nothing more than domestic animals to many of the rich and the officials in power. Hongwu did not believe in allowing laws to be misinterpreted or misuse of the lower classes since he came from the peasant class. Hongwu had twenty-six sons. He named Zhu Biao his successor, except he died before Hongwu did.

Ming Xiaoling- Mausoleum of Hongwu

Zhu Yunwen

Zhu Yunwen or Emperor Jianwen was the grandson of Emperor Hongwu. Zhu Yunwen was born to Zhu Biao and named successor instead of the second eldest son. Unfortunately, Zhu Yunwen was only on the throne for four years before his uncles led the Jingnan Rebellion. Uncle Zhu Di, known as Emperor Yongle, became the third Emperor of the Ming Dynasty. Records are inconclusive about Zhu Yunwen's death or life after being ousted as Emperor.

Emperor Yongle

Chengzu or Yung Lo (Zhu Di) was known as the Yongle Emperor. He reigned from 1403 to 1424. Yongle also contributed significantly to the Ming Dynasty with his construction of the Forbidden City and reopening China to the world. His reign left China poor because of the construction projects and the seven voyages of Zheng He. Lack of funds made it difficult to face Mongol insurgents in the mid-fifteenth century.

Zheng He

Zheng He's (Ma He) family was Mongolian with Muslim ties. Prince Zhu Di, later Emperor Yongle, took Zheng He as a slave. Rising through the ranks, he became a trusted advisor.

He oversaw the Chinese Navy and explored Southeast Asia, the Middle East, and Africa, as the Chief Envoy. On a visit to Somalia, Zheng returned with a giraffe he gifted to the emperor. The journeys brought back goods from the Middle East and Africa, particularly from India, plus news of the world. Zheng He's voyages lowered the suspicion of foreigners who had to be part of the tribute system during Hongwu's reign.

Zheng was part of the tactics to take over Vietnam, while he also managed the troops sent to the northern borders to stop Mongols from retaking China. Yongle preferred peace and strategy by ensuring international relations were formed using Zheng He on diplomatic missions. Zheng became a eunuch to show he was no threat to the Emperor. Zheng supplied silk and Ming porcelain on his journeys west and enhanced the trading system.

Junk ship

Zheng used Junks, a type of large bottom ship of 400 feet long and 170 feet wide, to explore. The first voyage contained 200 ships, plus 28,000 men. The size enabled Zheng to bring back treasures and to carry horses and men. Ships in the fleet were specifically for carrying water. Zheng ran into pirates, visited Calicut India, and created diplomatic relations. The next six missions included visiting a total of twenty-five countries. He brought back diplomats to meet the emperor. Zheng He died on the seventh mission.

Zheng's main influence on other nations was information, versus getting them to believe China was the middle of the world and thus the Son of Heaven. Zheng brought news of foreign lands, customs, and gifts. Some historical text believes the missions were to root out Jianwen to prevent a possible overthrow.

Zheng He served Yongle, Hongxi, and Xuande, with the first six missions served under Yongle.

Reign of Yongle

Emperor Yongle was ruthless like his father regarding the bureaucracy. He killed any official who might have been loyal to Jianwen. He killed thousands, including Fang Xiaoru who refused to announce Yongle's Emperor status. Officials appointed by Xiaoru also died.

Like his father, Yongle created secret police, this time led by the head eunuch. He felt eunuchs were best for the positions because they could not have children and would be loyal to the emperor. The Eastern Depot (Bureau), a eunuch spy agency, routed out any legitimate ruler and corruption. To rid the world of information, Yongle ordered Jianwen's legitimate claims to the throne and his reign to be removed from the records.

The construction of the Forbidden City was two-fold: keep the north protected from Mongolian invasions and abandon the decimated former capital. The Forbidden City was built inside an enlarged Beijing and had nine gates. The Grand Canal was rebuilt to ensure ships could get to the capital with food. The imperial residence was inaccessible to anyone not approved by the Emperor, hence the name. The east side of the grand palace was for the Emperor and his men. The western area was for his wife, concubines, and children. Some officials and ambassadors of rank gained access to live within the walls.

The Forbidden City

Emperor Yongle requested work start on the *Yongle Canon* known as the *Yongle Dadian*. The

61

most massive and comprehensive history of Chinese literary works, the *Yongle Dadian* was created by 147 scholars and revised by over 3,000. It contains 22,000 chapters, plus 60 chapters for an index. Only 800 sections remain.

Emperor Yongle not only built the Forbidden City, repaired the Grand Canal, but he started to renovate the Great Wall to defend against the Mongols. Yongle died during a fifth campaign to stop Mongols, dying on the battlefield, leaving his son, Hongxi, to reign. Unfortunately, Hongxi died of a heart attack a year later, and Xuande, Yongle's grandson took over.

Emperor Zhu Zhanji

Zhu Zhanji took the name Xuande when he took the throne in 1426. Early in Zhu Zhanji's reign an uncle, Zhu Gaoxu, attempted to overtake Zhanji's position, but Zhanji ruled until his death in 1435. Xuande was known for bringing peace to China by safeguarding the borders, fighting off natural calamities that might have crippled the country, and patronizing the arts. Empress Dowager Zhang, his mother, was instrumental in Xuande's reign. She had to abdicate her position for being infertile. His wife, Empress Sun, provided two sons and two daughters. Xuande spent most of his time on arts, including increasing the manufacture of porcelain. He enjoyed luxury, precious stones, and unusual animals. Xuande did not think about his palace position as he should; instead, he chose not to eliminate political influence from former emperors and those fighting to take his power. The eunuchs had too much political power, and Xuande gave them military power.

The eunuchs captured Xuande's successor, ripped off the empire, amassed wealth, and used the secret society to slander and blackmail administrators and generals who stood in their way to power. Historians believe Xuande's rule began the end of the Ming Dynasty and thus the end of the Han imperial rule. The Han Dynasty (221-206) continued to influence China because the Han relatives ruled China; however, the last Han relative sat as emperor during the Ming Dynasty.

Zhengtong

Emperor Zhengtong, or Zhu Qizhen, reigned twice, the second time under the name of Tianshun. He ascended the throne during a period of strife when a eunuch, Wang Zhen, had the most power. Wang Zhen was instrumental in getting Zhengtong captured by Mongol forces because of his poor advice. Zhu Qiyu, as Emperor Jingtai, took over the reign. The accounts of Zhengtong's kidnapping differ. One resource says Emperor Zhengton remained captured for ransom for four years, and another says the kidnapping was only a year, but both agree no payment occurred. In 1457, Jingtai fell ill allowing Zhengtong to restore his throne for seven years (he died). Zhengtong was a puppet for the eunuchs even during his second reign.

Emperor Chenghua

Emperor Chenghua was Tianshun's son, and Chenghua's uncle, Jingtai, made his life difficult when he took the empty emperor's position during his father's kidnapping. Jingtai removed Chenghua's title of the crown prince, and any misstep could have taken his life. Chenghua took the throne in 1457 after Tianshun died. Emperor Chenghua was 17. He started replacing government policies, reducing taxes, and attempting to strengthen the Ming Dynasty. Later, a eunuch, Wang Zhi, rose to power. Peasants fought against the government and violence ensued. Emperor Chenghua created the Eastern and Western Depots to check civilians' words and actions, taking away their freedom.

Palace intrigue (plots against consorts, empresses, or the emperor) existed for many emperors, and consorts were instilled to gain power. Consort Wan was one of the women who gained power through the emperor. Consort Wan used eunuchs, was seventeen years older than Chenghua, and used this age difference be a mother figure which helped her gain power. Consort Wan used the eunuchs to gain information, to pass information, and basically to spy throughout the palace and China. Rumors state Consort Wan used palace staff, such as the eunuchs, to poison those who might try to grab power. Wan also used her family and education to outsmart councilors, other consorts, and power-hungry people.

She dominated the harem, gave birth to a son, Zhu Youcheng, and hid him away. Emperor Hongzhi, Zhu Youcheng, was raised outside the palace to protect him as the crown prince.

Chenghua's downfalls include being easily influenced, mainly, by Consort Wan, while trying to dominate individuals and the lower classes. The ruling class became wasteful, corrupt, and Ming was left destitute.

Emperor Hongzhi

Emperor Hongzhi (reign 1487-1505) had one empress and no consorts. Hongzhi returned the government to a more transparent one, encouraging the ministers to communicate on all issues. Scholars believe Emperor Hongzhi was among the most brilliant of emperors. Emperor Hongzhi spent the first five years of his life in hiding, then entered the palace to gain the best education possible. He focused on the Confucian principles by lowering taxes, removing corrupt officials, encouraging honesty and loyalty among ministers, and encouraging trade. Hongzhi knew the people were important and focused on their needs. Emperor Hongzhi welcomed constructive criticism, which helped the empire thrive.

Emperor Zhengde

Zhengde ruled from 1505 to 1521, as the eldest son of Emperor Hongzhi. Zhengde was raised to be kind and thoughtful, but instead, he neglected state affairs. He allowed eunuchs and military advisors to make decisions. He focused more on entertainment, women, and wine. Advisors to the Emperor pushed for contact with explorers to open trade with Chinese merchants which would help refill the coffers. He died at 30.

Emperor Jiajing (1521-1567)

Emperor Jiajing lasted longer than his immediate predecessors did on the throne; however, most chancellors did not like Jiajing. Emperor Zhengde died suddenly and had no heir, so Jiajing was chosen as a relation to the Imperial family. The Chinese required a direct descendant of the last emperor to take the throne, by adoption if necessary, but Jiajing declared his father emperor posthumously, gaining disfavor among the court. People who opposed him were tortured or executed. An assassination attempt on Jiajing failed and led to more executions.

Jiajing believed in Daoist thoughts and was known for being a cruel leader. Jiajing did not live in the Forbidden City but in isolation, allowing his eunuch advisors, Zhang Cong and Yan Song, to handle state affairs. Both men gained the power to make decisions in place of Jiajing, and eventually, Yan Song won more power than Cong, ensuring he was the man behind the emperor. Yan Song and Yan Shifan (his son) took over the government, killing ministers who spoke against them, and Jiajing ignored their behavior. Jiajing abandoned his duties entirely in 1539, refusing for nearly 25 years to hold court. He sent word through eunuchs and select loyal officials.

The corruption that started with Zhengde continued through Jiajing's reign.

Emperor Longqing

Son of Jiajing, Emperor Longqing took over in a tumultuous time reigning from 1567 to 1572. Longqing reformed the government by bringing in talented officials, namely Han Rui. He removed corrupt priests and established trade with Africa, Europe, and Asia. He fortified the seaports along the Fujian and Zhejiang coasts. Longqing is also known for the peace treaty with the Mongols who managed to get over the Great Wall and into Beijing. The treaty allowed the trade of silk for horses. Unfortunately, earlier rule changed to allow Meng Cong and other eunuchs to take over the inner court.

Emperor Wanli

Emperor Wanli had a monumental task when taking over as emperor, but he was only nine. He had to get help from Zhang Juzheng, a statesman and skilled administrator. During Wanli's ten years, the Ming Dynasty prospered. The military was strong, nearly as strong as during Emperor Yongle's reign. Fighting among the nobles almost led to Zhang dismissal, but he died before that happened. Wanli respected Zhang but hated the strict Confucian rules. On his death, Wanli took over attending morning court, listening to state affairs, and defending China against Japanese and Mongolian invasions. With 48 years on the throne and the last twenty in isolation, the eunuchs took Emperor Wanli's responsibilities. Scholars believe this change after the wars is what led to the Manchus gaining strength and eventually succeeding in taking over the Ming Dynasty in 1644.

The next two Emperors were not significant except to say one lasted a month and the other, Tianqi, for seven years, but he was illiterate, leaving the eunuchs in power.

Emperor Chongzhen

Chongzhen reigned from 1627 to 1644, making him the last emperor of the Ming Dynasty. He was the fifth son of Emperor Taichang and seventeen years old. Tianqi was his brother. Wei Zhongxian, a eunuch, continued in power until Chongzhen's official appointment. He killed the de facto rulers during his brother's reign. Chongzhen faced a destitute treasury, years of corruption, and a commanding general, Yuan Chonghuan. Yuan Chonghuan protected the northern border against the Manchus, but his death left Ming defenseless. Farmer uprisings due to famine, drought, and lack of government help ensured Ming was weak. Li Zicheng of the Manchus created a revolution, got past the guards at Beijing, and Emperor Chongzhen knew his rule was over. Chongzhen attempted to kill his daughters and concubines before the conquers could mistreat them. He climbed to Jing Mountain and hung himself rather than face execution.

Each emperor faced a challenge—to make Ming better or worse—overall throughout the centuries, some made drastic and progressive changes, while others reveled in entertainment and spending money.

The government structure went between a monarchy and trusted advisors to some advisors taking over to gain independent wealth and power. At times, emperors should have given control away and didn't, while others should have strived to follow the practices of their previous emperor. In nearly 300 years, peasants went from being relevant to being lowly citizens, ignored and abused, while trade flourished, coffers became full and then empty and conquers from other lands attempted war after war.

At any given time, China had over three hundred thousand government officials, advising, weighing in, and attempting to take control away from the emperors. Numbers dwindled during the massacres by various emperors and control over corruption occurred.

Palace intrigue increased the discord between emperors and government officials. Many of the empresses gained status through marriage, designed to get the emperor's attention as a method of gaining favor for the entire family. To say women were considered unimportant is a fact; however, women of nobility and married into power typically had the ear of their husbands and could make suggestions. Rumors say empresses and consorts plotted assassinations of other consorts, empresses, and even emperors. Killing heirs to put another on the throne is mainly supposition, but evidence found by scholars indicates the early deaths of emperors' children could be related to poisoning over poor health, illness, and poor conditions in life. At least one execution of an empress occurred because she attempted to overthrow the government and upset the well-liked consort.

The Military

The military was an inherited job for many soldiers in the "warrior class." Warriors were low in social status, usually peasants who did not become farmers. Morale was low, with the only motivation being survival. When a soldier died, his family provided the next able-bodied man. Families who refused to send a man to replace their dead loved one, ended up stripped of their livelihood and had to become beggars. Soldiers equated to "cannon fodder," men who went out to be killed to protect the true fighters and generals.

The infantry, low-class soldiers, made up 112 men to a regiment (a section of military troops). Units included infantry and specialists. The specialist soldiers made up 40% of the regiment, handling weapons like crossbows and firearms. Another 20% of the group had swords and shields.

Cavalry troops (horseback riders) had archers and lancers with shields. Lancers would charge with their horses and weapons hoping to break the enemies' formations enough to weaken them.

Centralized planning was a notable tactic by Ming military, where the army would be re-equipped, retrained for specific campaigns. The limitations included bureaucracy interference ensuring a slower response to immediate threats. Troops used for non-military reasons reduced battle readiness and military might.

Author Sun Tzu is known for the *Art of War*, a book that describes the military-style way to wage wars successfully, yet the Ming military was lacking in many things, including strategy against the Mongols, Japanese, and Vietnamese. The massive numbers of men, due to the extensive overpopulation of China, helped ensure plenty of soldiers could be pulled from their homes to fight against an invasion.

Chapter 4: Travel and Trade by Silk Road

Everyday life was about survival for all classes, although the lower classes had to worry about surviving more than the aristocrats. For nobles, if they did not attempt a coup or speak ill of the current emperor, they would survive. Slaves carried palanquins or drove carriages for nobles. A palanquin is a large box with two horizontal poles. Four to six men would carry the boxes, which held one person. Some nobles had open palanquins, which are more like chairs than boxes. Military, government officials, and high-class citizens owned horses for other modes of travel. Peasants and merchants rarely had the income to own horses, let alone ride them. Merchants used pack animals, such as camels, for trade. Large caravans included guards and merchants, the more people in a group, the easier for everyone to defend against bandits who would steal goods.

Palanquin

Travel along roads was by caravan; particularly, the Silk Road. The Silk Road started during the Han Dynasty (206 BC -220 AD). Peak travel was during the Yuan Dynasty; however, when the various emperors closed sea trade to merchants, the Silk Road became an integral part of travel and trade again.

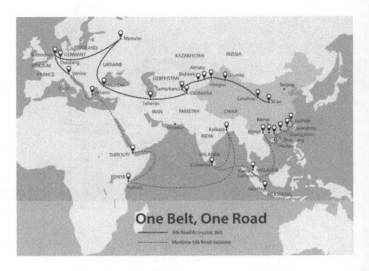

One Belt, One Road, Chinese strategic investment in the 21st century map

Silk Road Facts

The Silk Road is 4,000 miles long.

- The Black Death (Bubonic Plague) traveled from Europe to Asia along the Silk Road.
- Merchants traveled only portions of the Silk Road.
- Merchants traded goods at cities and trading posts.

- More than one route existed, some with shorter and more dangerous passages.

The Silk Road ran from China to Eastern Europe. The road was along the northern borders of China, India, and Persia and ended in Turkey at the Mediterranean Sea. Turkey was part of the Ottoman Empire.

The nomenclature, "Silk Road," came from the trading of silk. Silk was a prized item in Asia and Europe to the point the Romans called China the "land of silk." China traded tea, salt, sugar, spices, and porcelain Europe could not access and imported gold, cotton, wool, ivory, and silver. Sweet potatoes arrived by Silk Road.

China did not trade bronze, but China is the first culture associated with the metal. Early dynasties used bronze coins for money, and Emperor Hongwu replaced the coins with paper money made of parchment. Foreign exchange of metal or paper currency did not exist between countries. Products traded for other goods through a bargaining system based on supply and demand. Current demand, previous years' costs, and current supplies determined the suggested value of the products.

Silver and gold became in-demand by nobles, and the "greed" for the precious metals ensured merchants had more than material items like cotton and wool to sell to upper classes.

Walking with animals loaded heavily with goods to trade made travel slow. Traveling 4,000 miles to trade would mean years on the Silk Road for just one trip, which is why merchants traveled only portions of the road. Merchants would bring items from China to a city or trading post, trade their goods for other items, and return. The next leg of merchants would trade along another part of the route, and on until the goods made their way to Eastern Europe. At the same time, traders from Eastern Europe would travel portions of the road to exchange their goods, keeping the supply chain open and in constant flux.

The timing for trades depended on the weather and prearranged markets. Traders had to make specific markets or risk returning with their goods unsold or ruined. Using more dangerous routes occurred when the timing was tight.

Illness and the Silk Road

Diseases of unknown causes affected millions all over the world. Chinese medicine believes in a theory of Yin and Yang, where the body must balance the two to remain healthy. In Europe, bloodletting, poking a vein and letting the blood run out, was considered the way to make someone survive the illness.

Unsanitary conditions, such as outhouses, lack of bathing, and no hand washing led to disease. Flooding brought on stomach ailments and contaminated water from poor conditions led to cholera.

The Bubonic Plague came from rodents carrying bacteria. The symptoms appeared flu-like, but with deadly consequences. Symptoms included fever, vomiting, headaches, pus-filled lesions, and eventually, death. Europe suffered thousands of deaths; one dark period became known as the Black Death. An infected person traveling along the Silk Road could spread the disease to his caravan and any other caravans met along the way. The epidemic reached China due to trade.

Trade System

Before a foreign exchange system, where one currency trades for another, trade meant goods for goods. A merchant could set a price for rice, such as three lengths of cotton for one bag of rice. The merchant with the cotton could agree or bargain.

People regulated bartering. Three parties, or a triangular barter, could occur, such as cotton traded for silk, traded for a camel. The price of a good was set based on supply and demand but in keeping with the previous year. A lower supply of rice would increase the amount one had to trade for the item. The demand also changed year to year, such as more westerners wanting silk. Regulators, higher class merchants, or court diplomats set the costs for goods.

Government officials needed to regulate trade to keep prized goods coming into their country. Emperors, upon the advice of counsel, set taxes, such as ten bags of rice. In unfavorable economic times, peasants and merchants had to increase the amount paid for taxes, creating a lower supply between other nations.

Closing trade to the West by ship impacted China's economy and trade. Use of the Silk Road fluctuated between bans on sea trade and open sea trade. When emperors allowed sea trade, travel along the Silk Road became nearly non-existent.

Supply and demand still affected trade, and the attempts to win over the emperor affected who made it through the military to dock in the ports. The more goods brought without thought of reciprocal trade on the trip, the better for merchants. The Portuguese were adept at bringing tributes and discussing fair trade to the point they earned Macau, a small island off China's coast, as their land. Other countries were not as successful. Emperors treated Westerners with suspicion, many thinking they had ulterior motives such as conquering China, and strife between Japan, Mongolia, and Vietnam did not help. The politics in the palace greatly affected trade routes and products for trade, which created issues for merchants.

Merchants grew rich and poor, depending on current world views. During Zheng He's seven missions, the government gained more than the low-class merchants. Merchant regulation affected the trading system by imposing taxes and restrictions. The first concept of "business licenses" limited the number of merchants who traded by land or sea.

Trade Production

The Han Dynasty began privatization of industries like tea and salt. The Ming Dynasty capitalized on the Han Dynasty economy, making vast improvements to agriculture, technology, manufacturing, and trade. Ming emperors used forced labor, paying wages to workers in factories. The Ming Dynasty had over 300 factories to craft pots and porcelain products for trade.

Agriculturally, crop rotation near the main rivers enhanced output for tea, fruits, rice, millet, and other grains. Cash crops like tea, rice, and fruits enabled the markets to run successfully. Rural, urban, and national markets existed, where the rural markets helped support farmers, and urban markets sold food and imported goods.

Trade became a thing of commerce and investments. One source states over 300 million silver pieces entered China due to trade. Silver taels (chunks of silver in an oval shape) and gold bricks became the trade in later Ming periods.

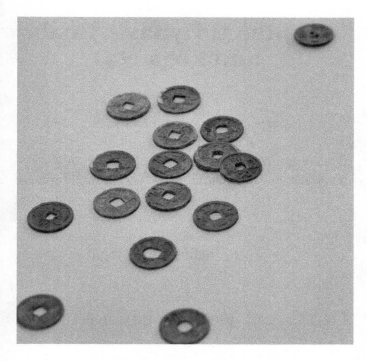

Ancient coin in brown background

The trade of products for goods ended towards the 1500s when silver and gold became the world currency. China strived to bring as much silver and gold into the country as possible and rarely traded it to other countries like Japan or Korea. The Ming Dynasty was an era where paper money became backed by gold and silver reserves.

Chapter 5: Dynasty Goals and Projects

Each Emperor had goals, some ensuring the Ming Dynasty's great reign, while others led to the dynasty's downfall. Massive projects impacted everyday life, government coffers, and the overall strength of the dynasty. Goals such as protecting the peasants and lowering the merchant population, trading via sea, and adding to the arts and entertainment defined an emperor's ruling style.

The Great Wall of China

The Great Wall of China

During the Ming Dynasty, the Great Wall of China gained 5,500 miles to became one long, connected wall of 13,171 miles by the end of the dynasties. Qin Shi Huang, Emperor of the Qin Dynasty, started construction on one long wall instead of the individual pieces the wall was in when he took control. The Ming Dynasty added more miles, keeping the construction Qin developed.

Peasants, criminals, slaves, and other men helped build the wall. Soldiers also helped build the wall and managed the lower ranks. Over 1,000 years, millions of people worked on the wall, and about a million died during the construction. Scientists and archeologists found the bones of those who died inside the wall. Workers used the bodies of the dead for material to support the stone structure.

Builders used resources around the area, such as dirt, bodies, and stone, but during the Ming Dynasty bricks replaced the haphazard materials. The wall protected the northern border, mainly from the Mongols. On top of the walls, watchtowers were built to send up signals and house the soldiers. Garrisons cropped up near the walls for soldiers to be on hand in case of an attack.

Interior of a watchtower

Wall Facts

- Seven thousand towers are part of the wall.
- Sections of the wall are eroding.

Erosion of the Great Wall

- The height and width vary, but the wall averages 33 feet tall and 15 feet wide, due to Ming construction.
- Moats also surrounded the wall during the Ming Dynasty.
- Smoke signals could be seen from tower to tower to alert of an invasion.
- The wall extends over desert, plains, and mountains.
- The highest point is 5,000 feet above sea level.

Scientists believe the wheelbarrow, an invention of the Chinese, helped during the construction of the wall.

Forbidden City Project

The Forbidden City

Emperor Yongle began the Forbidden City, but the Qing added more to the palace. Over one million people helped construct the palace, using only the best materials, since the palace was for the emperor. Books refer to the materials as "golden" bricks, marble, and trees. Logs came from Phoebe Zhen nan trees. Yellow tiles create the roof because the color is associated with ultimate power. No one could wear yellow—yellow was the emperor's color—along with red.

Yellow roof

Palace Facts

- The palace covers 178 acres.
- Ninety-eight individual palaces exist behind the walls.
- A total of 980 buildings complete the complex.
- More than 8,700 various rooms with a total floor space of 1,600,000 square feet make up the palace. The area equates to 28 football fields.
- The palace structural design is meaningful to Chinese culture.

- Ceremonial buildings occur in groups of three since the number represents heaven in Chinese culture.
- Nine and five are also crucial to the Chinese and represent the majesty of the monarchy.
- The palace design has white, red, black, yellow, and green for important colors.
- Black represents water; thus, the library roof is black to "prevent and protect" against fire.

The layout of the palace design and many homes in ancient China have special symbolism. The Forbidden City was more than home to the emperors; the palace was a symbol to the world showing strength, superiority, and beliefs.

Building placement lined up north to south with entrances on the southern side. Two sections, the inner and outer court, were built. The palace, although a residence, was mainly a fortress against the Mongolians and other warring factions (invading countries).

Walls, twenty-six feet high, surround the palace. The moat, one hundred seventy feet wide, no longer exists. Nine gates allowed entry with the main gate was the Meridian at the south. Other gates include the Gate of Divine Might, West Glorious Gate, and East Glorious Gate.

The Gate of Divine Might, on the north, was named to show strength. For holiness, buildings and entrances faced south. The north, with Mongol aggressors, had cold winds and "evil."

Gate of Divine Might

The outer court managed official ceremonies, with the Hall of Preserving Harmony, Hall of Supreme Harmony, and Hall of Central Harmony. The emperors held court in the Hall of Supreme Harmony.

Throne in the Hall of Preserving Harmony

The personal wing of the palace was the inner court and placed in the northern section of the Forbidden City. The Emperor lived in the Palace of Heavenly Purity. The Empresses resided in the Palace of Earthly Tranquility.

Throne in the Palace of Heavenly Purity

Today, the palace is a museum housing thousands of artifacts and art from various dynasties, including some of the best Ming porcelain pieces. No one, without extremely special permission, is allowed into the Emperor quarters or the Hall of Preserving Harmony; however, one can view the room by standing outside the roped off area. *The Last Emperor*, a movie, was able to film inside the palace.

93

The Grand Canal

The Grand Canal

The third project during the Ming Dynasty, the Grand Canal, was a renovation goal. The canal connects the Yellow and Yangtze rivers. Both rivers impacted trade getting supplies from the coast to the Forbidden Palace. The Grand Canal is the longest human-made waterway anywhere in the world, stretching 1,100 miles from Beijing to Hangzhou. The Ming Dynasty floated boats loaded with grain from the south to Beijing to feed the city residents, Emperor and his family, and soldiers.

The first canal, started in 480 BC by King Fuchai, went from the Yangtze River to the Huai. The

Hong Guo Canal on the Yellow River connected to the Bian River which helped with early trade. The Grand Canal connected both canals into one long waterway.

Emperor Yang (Shi Dynasty) used farmers to construct the main canal circa 609 AD, and the Ming emperors improved it. New locks, reservoirs, and deeper sections ensured better travel along the rivers.

Canal Facts

- Emperors traveled on the canal to inspect the locks.
- The Ming Dynasty used 45,000 full-time laborers and thousands of part-time peasants for the construction.
- The government operated more than 11,000-grain barges during the Ming Dynasty.
- The canal helped the government collect taxes.

Inventions Paved the Way for Ming

Paper, printing, silk, the compass, gunpowder, and boat rudders existed before the Ming Dynasty; however, the dynasty would improve these works. Paper appeared in the second century BC and became part of the manufactured goods by 105 AD. Woodblock printing, a popular form of art today, was invented in 868 AD and enhanced as a moveable type two hundred years later. Gutenberg, a European inventor of the printing press, was late to the concept—China beat him to the invention with the moveable type invention.

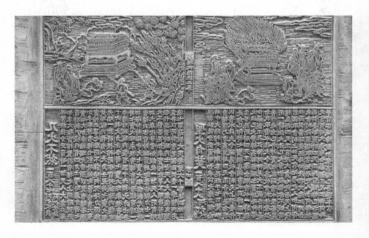

Carved woodblock.

Documents were mass produced in two colors during the Ming Dynasty. Workers carved woodblocks, which became part of a moveable type mechanism producing two-color ink.

Silk

Silk Cocoons with Worm

Silk comes from silkworms that create cocoons. Early Chinese dissected the cocoons to figure out how to spin the silk into clothing. The process of making silk remained a secret for hundreds of years, giving the export value. The Ming Dynasty is responsible for the invention of silk and cotton looms.

The Compass

Chinese inventors made the magnetic compass. Cities formed based on compass points, and then the tool became essential for ship navigation.

Gunpowder

Chemists in the ninth century AD discovered gunpowder. Gunpowder led to the invention of fireworks, bombs, mines, guns, and rockets. Chemists attempted to find the "Elixir of Immortality" and found combustible powder instead.

Ship Rudders

The rudder appeared in 200 AD; however, the Ming Dynasty improved the invention to help steer large ships into deep waters. The rubber made its way from China to the rest of the world.

Toothbrush

AD 1498 marks the year of the toothbrush. Before the toothbrush, sticks with flared edges, called chew sticks, kept teeth clean. Pig bristles replaced the sticks, and the toothbrush became refined from the early Ming concept.

Other inventions, improved during the Ming Dynasty, include the wheelbarrow, umbrella, iron casting, kites, matches, stirrups, and porcelain. A military technological achievement put science together with the army to create the Huochong Gun which measured 105 mm and weighed 6.94 kilograms. It used gunpowder to force a projectile through the bronze tube. The gun was a straight tube much like a canon, but small enough to hold.

Weapons of mass destruction, such as the Gatling gun of later centuries, came into fruition (were invented) because of the Chinese work with gunpowder and metal. Winchester, Remington, and other American gun manufacturers took over the prowess of gun creation because the Chinese shared their information about gunpowder and using metal to power a projectile into another living being. Before guns, swords, made of lightweight metals, often with curved blades, and lances protected the Chinese from invaders.

Chapter 6: How the Ming Dynasty Impacted Today's Society

The Ming Dynasty started because of one man and his rebel army were tired of tyranny and oppression. Hongwu shows us, one man, with enough influence, can rise against an emperor and government that kills because it can. Genghis Khan wanted to rule China. Kublai Khan fulfilled Genghis' wish ruling China in his stead. We see some of the same traits occurring today, with countries fighting wars to overtake another or to unseat a regime rebels dislike. The difference, though, is technology, inventions, and a belief of better values today.

China, the Ming Dynasty especially, influenced today's society with their inventions, culture, and certain government elements. Ship rudders, guns, the compass, paper, manufactured typesetting, and furniture arrangement hail from improvements made during the Ming Dynasty.

The rulers show us what should and should not be done, although we may not listen to the lessons of the past. Emperor Hongwu showed the world a low born man could rise to a successful, prominent position without losing his morals. Did he kill indiscriminately? Morally, he killed many people under suspicion of corruption, without solid proof, yet, he raised peasant status attempting to oust the wealthy from positions of honor to ensure a loyal and hardworking government.

Other emperors wasted money, ignored government laws, and even rejected the court leaving the power in the hands of eunuchs to oppress, kill, and spread corruption tamped out by Hongwu and a few other Ming emperors. The downfall of the Ming Dynasty was overspending, overpopulation, and corruption. Emperors of the 1500s and 1600s opened chasms that could not be plugged by new rulers who were serious about correcting the corruption.

The tale of the Ming is not a new one, for any empire, as seen by Egyptians, Roman, and Ottoman rulers. Greed, disinterest, and disloyalty infiltrated ruling entities until they imploded, leaving themselves open to new rulers and governments. China did not fall because of the Ming Dynasty, even the Qing who lost power in the early 1900s against Japan and World War I could not end China. Although China became weak for much of the 1900s, the government lessons from the Ming and other dynasties have helped it survive and become a powerful nation again.

Overpopulation is still a problem. Throughout the 1900s, women were considered less and abandoned or adopted into Western cultures, but many women are starting to hold important positions.

Today, communism reigns, keeping oppression a considerable part of society, with specific thoughts and ideas allowed, while others are blocked. China continues its view as the center of Heaven, ensuring outside news and influences remain blocked. Websites, search engines, and apps the Western nations use without thought are not available in China. China has their inventions in technology and social media designed to limited exposure to "world" corruption.

The government limits education, jobs, and vehicle ownership. Vehicle ownership is due to keeping pollution at a minimum. Millions of people live in China, and if each one had a car, the roadways would be bumper to bumper in cities, pollution would be worse than Los Angeles, and Chinese regard nature as imperative. Low carbon footprints, with the use of bicycling everywhere, is vital to the government and the people. Skills, test scores, and proof of intelligence allow people to gain more freedoms.

The rituals and beliefs of China influence business deals. Bowing is a sign of respect, and the deeper the bow to a person of higher importance, the more respect one shows. Negotiations are handled in boardrooms, with particular rules and rituals to show respect. Ming political structure influences business with outside companies and other countries to decrease foreign influences and increase investments. Importing goods from the world helps bring food sources and other necessary products into China; however, China exports a great deal more than it introduces.

Statistics from 2018 show there is a trade surplus with the US, with a 17 percent growth year to year. Exports to the US rose by 11.3 percent, while imports into China from the US only increased by 0.7 percent. A trade surplus shows the value of the exports exceeds the value of the imports, meaning China sent more goods to the US than they brought into their country. From an economic standpoint, a country wants a trade surplus because it keeps more money in their banks.

The Ming Dynasty had periods of growth and weakness. Emperors who spent too much on improvements, art, entertainment, and military coups sent China into a struggle versus the Ming emperors who traded for profit without overspending.

The US carries a deficit, meaning the US owes several countries, including China, money for investment funds. The empty coffers can only fill when more exports leave the country than money spent bringing in imports. Another way is to provide loans; however, the US, in the last decade, needed loans versus being able to lend money to other countries. Economically, the US has become Ming China during Emperor Zhengde's reign. Too much money goes out, with wasted relations, sparking instability.

Focusing solely on China and Chinese society, Christianity, Buddhism, Taoism, and Confucianism exists, with an overwhelming government. Public ownership of property occurs under communism's theory. Correlating this to the Ming Dynasty, only during Hongwu's reign, fallow land became fruitful, and peasants could own property. During the Ming Dynasty, each person had a job and payment was based on his or her abilities and the country's needs, which fits the communist way of thinking.

Families receive supplies based on their work and needs. Families are kept small, with one offspring, preferably male, to keep the family going. Multi-generations still live in one home together, although many young married couples are starting to find apartments rather than stay in their family homes.

Schooling is merit-based like the Ming Dynasty of Hongwu's reign. Private school is available for families who can afford it, including sending children to other countries to learn their ways, government, and social structure, to improve life in China. You can think of foreign exchange students as modern-day explorers gaining knowledge and bringing back the essential lessons.

China Facts

- Xiongan is a new city in China; a "modern, green, and livable" city according to news sources. Xiongan is twice the size of Manhattan and 100 km from Beijing. By 2025, 200 cities in China will have more than 1 million people.
- China is spending $1.3 billion to convert to electric power to improve the quality of life.

- The last coal-fired power station was closed, making China a coal-free nation for electricity and heating.
- China has the world's second-largest economy.
- Technology in China is vast, with QI codes used for many purchases, information lookups, or even rentals.
- China invests in renewable energy, solar power, and has the largest solar farm in the world. A solar farm is a field, in China's case, a floating farm, of nothing but linked solar panels to harness the energies sun.

Solar farm

- China makes the most substantial amount of goods the world buys by filing for more patents than any country or person in the world. Intellectual property rights, patents for inventions, rose to 45% in 2016, which keeps it close to US and Japanese patents on file.
- Artificial Intelligence is a leading research industry.

The facts show China has continued making discoveries, inventions, and retains their status as a leading country.

Conclusion

The Ming Dynasty lasted for 276 years, with more than ten Emperors influencing the government and social structure to help formulate the Chinese culture and economic power we see today. The Ming Dynasty shows periods of extreme growth, wealth, and poverty due to wars, natural disasters, and greed.

Power struggles gave and took control from emperors, whether by force or pure ignorance. Eventually, the Ming Dynasty came to a halt due to spying, power grabs, and disinterest in the throne, allowing a new era to enter and gain more domination of surrounding countries and trade.

Lasting impressions from the Ming include inventions like guns, ship rudders, wheelbarrows, and agricultural technology. Improving the canals, opening sea trade, and investments in Eastern Europe helped bring growth to China while paving the way for continued success more than four centuries later.

More from us

CPSIA information can be obtained
at www.ICGtesting.com
Printed in the USA
LVHW101959120522
718626LV00007B/1270